BALOCH NATIONALISM
AND THE GEOPOLITICS
OF ENERGY RESOURCES:
THE CHANGING CONTEXT OF SEPARATISM
IN PAKISTAN

Robert G. Wirsing

*****

Comments pertaining to this report are invited and should be forwarded to: Director, Strategic Studies Institute, U.S. Army War College, 122 Forbes Ave, Carlisle, PA 17013-5244.

*****

ROBERT G. WIRSING is a member of the faculty of the Asia-Pacific Center for Security Studies, Honolulu, Hawaii. A specialist on South Asian politics and international relations, he has made over 40 research trips to the South Asian region since 1965. His recent research focuses primarily on the politics and diplomacy of natural resources (water and energy) in South Asia. Dr. Wirsing's publications include *Pakistan's Security under Zia, 1977-1988* (St. Martin's Press, 1991); *India, Pakistan, and the Kashmir Dispute* (St. Martin's Press, 1994); *Kashmir in the Shadow of War* (M. E. Sharpe, 2002); *Religious Radicalism & Security in South Asia*, co-editor (Asia-Pacific Center for Security Studies, 2004); and *Ethnic Diasporas & Great Power Strategies in Asia*, co-editor (India Research Press, 2007).

SUMMARY

This monograph examines the Baloch separatist insurgency that has resurfaced in recent years in Pakistan's sprawling Balochistan province. The author maintains that the context of today's insurgency differs in certain important respects from that of its 1970s predecessor. Most fundamental of these differences are those stemming from energy resource developments in what some are calling the "Asian Middle East" (embracing parts of South, Central, and Southwest Asia). In particular, the monograph looks at how Pakistan's mounting energy insecurity—a product of rapid increase in demand coupled with rising scarcity and the region's intensified energy rivalry— has magnified the economic and strategic importance of Balochistan, while at the same time complicating Pakistan's efforts to cope with the province's resurgent tribal separatism.

This change in the energy context exerts a powerful threefold impact on the insurgents' prospects. In the first place, it lifts Balochistan and Baloch nationalism to a position much higher on the scale of central government priorities, thus seeming to warrant, as the government sees the problem, zero tolerance and ruthless crushing of the insurgency. Second, it arms the Baloch insurgents both with greater incentives than ever for reclaiming control of Balochistan and with the novel capacity to drive the economic and political costs to the government of continuing insurgent activity far higher than ever in the past. Third (and on a more hopeful note), by promising to turn Balochistan into an important corridor for energy trafficking in the region, the changed context creates major opportunities for addressing Baloch nationalist demands in a positive and peaceful manner. While conceding that the counterinsurgency strategy pursued by the government thus far has a conspicuously dark side, the author insists that Balochistan's rapidly changing energy context could supply both the means and the incentives for bringing the insurgency to a swift, negotiated, and amicable end.

It is recognized that getting the Pakistan government to reverse course in Balochistan—and to engage the Baloch nationalists politically instead of only militarily—will no be easy. It is not just that a presumed force-reliant military "mindset" will get in the way; the problem of resolving Balochistan's political fortunes is much more complicated than that.

Today a formidable array of energy-related and other strategic forces impinge on that part of the world. As in the 1970s, Balochistan still falls in the shadow of strife-torn Afghanistan, which confronts Islamabad with an endless source of policy dilemmas. However, innumerable other shadows, equally problematic and all with their own set of imperatives, have now been added. The monograph highlights the manner, in particular, in which Pakistan's energy imperatives crowd in upon its policymaking in regard to the circumstances in Balochistan. These imperatives include not only its own natural gas resources, but also the proposed import of natural gas from Iran and/or Turkmenistan and its all-important collaboration with China in the laying of groundwork for a north-south commercial and energy corridor. It seems highly unlikely that these imperatives will grow any less pressing as time goes on. As a consequence, persuading the government to give significantly higher priority to accommodation of the Baloch tribal minority will unquestionably be a hard sell.

BALOCH NATIONALISM AND THE GEOPOLITICS OF ENERGY RESOURCES: THE CHANGING CONTEXT OF SEPARATISM IN PAKISTAN

Introduction.

In Afghanistan's Shadow, a book published in 1981 by well-known author Selig S. Harrison, examined that era's threat of Soviet expansionism in the light of Baloch nationalism. It was in Balochistan,[1] the vast and sparsely populated province in southwestern Pakistan, that the Pakistan army had ruthlessly suppressed a tribal separatist insurgency in the course of the 1970s. Rebellious Balochistan lay between Afghanistan and the sea. Since Soviet forces had militarily occupied Afghanistan in late 1979, the possibility had naturally arisen that Soviet leaders might be tempted to realize the long-cherished Russian goal of securing a warm-water port by exploiting lingering separatist grievances in neighboring Pakistan. "A glance at the map," Harrison wrote at the outset of his book, "quickly explains why strategically located Balochistan and the five million Baloch tribesmen who live there could easily become the focal point of superpower conflict."[2]

Over a quarter-century has passed since Harrison made that observation. Baloch nationalism is again on the rise, and Balochistan is again the scene of violent encounters between Baloch militants and Pakistani security forces. Not surprisingly, in comparing today's insurgency[3] with its 1970s forerunner, we find numerous continuities. Conspicuous among them are the government's persistent refusal to concede any legitimacy to Baloch nationalism or to engage the Baloch nationalists in serious political negotiations. These refusals run in company with its parallel tendency to secure its aims in Balochistan mainly by military means.

No less evident, however, are the discontinuities between the earlier and current episodes of Baloch insurgency. These discontinuities have arisen because the context of today's conflict in both its external and internal domains has in the meantime undergone some obvious transformation. The Soviet Union is no more. Shrunken Russia's historical quest for a warm-water port now seems barely conceivable and is rarely discussed. American and North Atlantic Treaty Organization (NATO) forces have taken the place of Soviet troops in Afghanistan, and today the Afghan enemies of these Western forces, in more than a few instances, are drawn from the ranks of what were at one time their staunch anti-Soviet allies. In the 1970s, Pakistan was just recovering from a disastrous military defeat suffered at the hands of India. It today manages to sustain a comprehensive dialogue with India aimed ostensibly at permanent peace and resting on a surprisingly successful ceasefire in Kashmir that marked its fourth anniversary near the end of 2007. The 1970s episode of Baloch insurgency featured the elected civilian-led government of Zulfikar Ali Bhutto as the militants' principal antagonist. In the current round of fighting, the Baloch nationalists are squared off against the army-dominated government of President Pervez Musharraf, who seized power in 1999.[4] The cast of characters in today's confrontation thus has clearly undergone major modification and role reversal, and the political and strategic motivations currently driving actions in the region are not simply copies of what they were in the earlier period. It is this change in the context of Baloch separatist nationalism that is examined in this monograph.

One of the most remarkable changes pertinent to today's conflict, and the particular focus of this monograph, has taken place in its energy context. Put simply, assured access to hydrocarbon or other energy resources, including both oil and natural gas, has in recent decades assumed a far greater importance than hitherto as a driver of Pakistan's security policy, both domestic and external. This is to say that energy security in Pakistan, as in most other countries in its neighborhood, now stands at or near the top of national priorities.[5]

A sizable hint of energy's gathering importance to the conflict in Balochstan was, of course, already apparent decades ago in the pages of Harrison's book. "If it were not for the strategic location of Baluchistan *and the rich potential of oil, uranium, and other resources,*" he observed, "it would be difficult to imagine anyone fighting over this bleak, desolate, and forbidding land."[6] But what was then a mere hint has taken on Himalayan proportions, exerting weight both in government and among the separatists that is often decisive.

With the gradual mounting of tensions between Baloch nationalists and the central government in the last 5 years have come frequent acts of anti-state violence, a substantial portion of them directed against the province's energy infrastructure and personnel. Pakistan's energy resources are thus tangibly implicated in the insurgency. Considered more closely, they have a direct and important relationship to Baloch nationalism in at least three ways. One is that Balochistan itself — the largest, least populated, and least developed of Pakistan's four provinces — is rich in energy resources.

Among the many grievances expressed by the Baloch nationalists, the most persistent and long-standing has been that these resources, including coal as well as gas, have been exploited by the central government without adequate compensation to the province.

A second way is that Balochistan is a transit site for major proposed natural gas pipelines that would carry gas from either Iran or Turkmenistan to Pakistan and from there potentially to India. One of many obstacles to the implementation of these pipeline projects has been the threat of Baloch militant attacks to disrupt gas supplies.

A third way in which energy resources have a direct and important relationship to Baloch nationalism is that Balochistan is the site of a major port facility and energy hub currently under development at Gwadar on the province's coast (see Map 1). Gwadar is the terminus of a projected interstate transport corridor that is to link Pakistan by road, rail, air, and, to some extent, pipeline with both China's Xinjiang province and, via Afghanistan, with the energy-rich Central Asian Republics (CARs). Baloch nationalists have complained that the government is developing the port and corridor without consultation with, involvement of, or benefit to the Baloch. The anger of Baloch nationalists has sometimes been directed against China, whose investment in the Gwadar project and in other Balochistan-based ventures has been substantial. A number of Chinese nationals have been the target of five violent attacks in Pakistan in recent years, with three of these attacks taking place in Balochistan, two of which resulted in fatalities.[7] Moreover, the additional fact that the port is being constructed to serve Pakistan's huge ambition to become a major energy resource and commercial trade intermediary on the Arabian Sea lends this grievance especial geo-strategic salience.

Map 1. Proposed Natural Gas Pipeline Routes Transiting Balochistan.

Obviously, the changed energy context exerts a strong influence on the tactical ebb and flow of the insurgent-counterinsurgent dynamic. But beyond this, the argument is made in this monograph that the changed energy context also exerts a powerful threefold impact on Baloch nationalism itself. First, it vastly increases the importance of Balochistan and Baloch nationalism to the central government. This increased importance is evident in the compounding pressures on government to bring the insurgency to a swift and definitive closure, the reinforcement of government's deep-seated intolerance of insurgent demands, and the growing temptation to settle the matter with brute force. Second, the changed energy context simultaneously arms the Baloch insurgents with greater incentives than ever for reclaiming control of Balochistan and, even more important, with the capacity to drive the economic and political costs of the government's counterinsurgency effort far higher than ever in the past. Third, to both sides' advantage, the changed energy context, which includes the potential for major increases in Pakistan's revenues and dramatic improvements in Balochistan's economy and social infrastructure, also supplies novel and abundant opportunities to address Baloch nationalist demands in a positive and mutually acceptable manner. Thus, while the insurgency unquestionably has its dark sides, its rapidly expanding energy context may supply the means to bring the insurgency to a negotiated and amicable end.

This monograph begins with a closer look at the energy-insurgency nexus.

Energy Geopolitics I: Balochstan's Energy Resources.

Balochistan has sizable reserves of coal and natural gas, and there is speculation that it may also hold large reserves of petroleum. At the moment, however, it is the province's natural gas that has special importance in Pakistan's energy profile. There are three reasons for its importance. One is that natural gas, accounting for about 50 percent of Pakistan's total energy consumption, is currently the country's principal energy source. Indeed, Pakistan's economy is one of the world's most natural gas dependent. The second is that, of Pakistan's proven natural gas reserves—in 2006 estimated at 28 trillion cubic feet (tcf)—as much as 19 trillion tcf (68 percent) are located in Balochistan. The third is that Balochistan accounts for from 36 to 45 percent of Pakistan's natural gas production, but consumes only a modest 17 percent of it.[8] Of particular note is that the largest share of the province's contribution to the nation's natural gas production comes from the long-operating Sui gas fields in the Bugti tribal domain, located among the parts most seriously afflicted by Baloch militancy.

The militant nationalists' capability to either block or disrupt the operations of the natural gas industry is clearly considerable, constituting a genuine threat, not a mere nuisance. The state-owned Sui Southern Gas Company alone, for instance, maintains a 27,542-kilometer pipeline distribution network, sprawling across the two provinces of Sindh and Balochistan, the size of which obviously defies continuous monitoring and policing.[9] According to reports compiled by writers for the Washington-based Jamestown Foundation, militant attacks and incidents of violence in general have become commonplace since the insurgency began escalating in 2002, and attacks against natural gas installations and pipelines in particular are steadily increasing in number. A January 2006 report stated that there had been

a total of 843 attacks and incidents of violence . . . reported in different parts of [Balochistan], including 54 attacks on law-enforcement agencies, 31 attacks on gas pipelines, 417 rocket attacks on various targets, 291 mine blasts, and 50 abductions. In the same period, a total of 166 incidents of violence were reported in the Kohlu [Marri tribal headquarters] district, including 45 bomb blasts and 110 rocket attacks. . . .[10]

A report by the same organization in late May 2006 declared that the violence had increased in frequency and intensity. "The favorite targets of insurgents," it explained,

> are energy production sites — such as Sui in Dera Bugti — and energy infrastructure that supplies natural gas to Pakistan's industrial hub in Punjab and Karachi. . . . On May 19, two main gas pipelines to Punjab were blown up, cutting off gas supplies to the province. . . . Although it is easy to damage Pakistan's extended but unguarded network of gas pipelines, insurgents are now hitting harder targets such as gas production sites.[11]

For Baloch nationalists, the over half-century history of Pakistan's domestic natural gas industry is one of unremitting indifference to the province's indigenous tribal population. When it came to jobs, for instance, the gas industry's well-paid managers and technicians were almost invariably drawn from outside Balochistan; local Baloch, inevitably viewed with some suspicion, were mainly employed in low-end jobs as day laborers.[12] An obvious remedy for the shortage of technically skilled Baloch qualified for employment in the gas industry — government funding of technical training institutions in Balochistan — was never seriously considered until recently.

The nationalists' strongest dissatisfaction is reserved, however, for what they term Balochistan's lopsidedly deficient share of revenues from the government's sale of natural gas. As it has evolved, the fiscal arrangement honoring provincial "ownership" of natural resources is fairly complex. Balochistan suffers from having been the first province in which gas was discovered. The royalty on natural gas paid by the central government to the provinces is based on wellhead production costs. These costs, since Balochistan's gas fields were discovered and developed much earlier than those in the Punjab and Sindh, were long ago stabilized and are today much less than in the other provinces. The result is that Balochistan receives proportionately only about one-fifth as much in royalty payments as the other two gas-producing provinces, a fiscal circumstance that has the ironic effect of turning Balochistan, the country's poorest province but leading supplier of gas, into an important subsidizer of the richer provinces.[13] The nationalists also maintain that historically very little of the huge earnings of the central government in natural gas revenues was ever returned to the province in the form of development expenditures.[14] In this, as will be discussed later in this monograph, they are undoubtedly correct.

Pakistan's annual consumption of natural gas, currently running at about 1 trillion cubic feet, is increasing at a fast pace at the same time that proven reserves are shrinking. This means that, apart from any increased reliance on imported supplies, pressure on Pakistan's natural gas resources coming from industrial, commercial, transport, and residential consumers is bound to increase. Some of that pressure can be relieved with more aggressive domestic exploration and extraction. But that avenue of relief could be negated by any production lost to militant strikes. The remedy there will have to come either by thoroughly crushing the militants or by striking a political bargain with them. That fact, in turn, guarantees that Pakistan's indigenous natural gas supplies, as long as they last, will remain a focal point of sharp controversy between Islamabad and Baloch nationalists.

Energy Geopolitics II: Natural Gas Pipelines.[15]

Two projects for transporting natural gas via
overland pipelines to markets in Pakistan and India
(see Map 1) are today being actively considered.
One is the proposed 2,700-kilometer-long (nearly
1,700-miles) Iran-Pakistan-India (IPI) pipeline with a
capacity to transport 2.8 billion cubic feet (bcf) of gas
daily from Iran's huge offshore South Pars field to
terminals in Pakistan and India. Estimated originally
to cost about $4 billion and more recently anywhere
from $7 to $9 billion, it has been under discussion since
the mid-1990s. The other project is the proposed 1,680-
kilometer-long (about 1,050-miles) Turkmenistan-
Afghanistan-Pakistan-India (TAPI) pipeline, with
cost estimates currently running somewhere between
$3.3 billion and $10 billion. This pipeline would have
the eventual capacity to transport up to 3.2 bcf daily
from Turkmenistan's Dauletabad field to markets in
Afghanistan, Pakistan, and, having been invited to join
the project in February 2006, India. In neither of the two
projects has the precise overland route of the pipeline
been decided, but both would transit Balochistan.
Energy experts are generally agreed that the
trilateral IPI project, which gained ground in 2004 with
the relaunching of the India-Pakistan peace process,
would bring enormous economic benefit to all three
countries involved—Iran, because the project would
help it bypass the U.S.-imposed and economically
painful Iran-Libya Sanctions Act of 1996 (renamed
by Congress the Iran Sanctions Act at the time of its
renewal in September 2006); India and Pakistan,
because in both countries energy supplies are falling
increasingly below energy demands.[16] Although the

three parties to the deal have shown positive signs in the past year or so of a determination to bring the project to fruition, the obstacles remain formidable and there are recent signs that the project may be on the brink of unraveling.

Spiraling costs of construction are one obstacle. Another is the price India would have to pay for the gas delivered at its border, which has to reflect consideration not only of Pakistani demands for a hefty customs tariff and transit fee but also of the potential for a more favorable price for gas delivered from India's own offshore Krishna Godavari (KG) natural gas fields in the Bay of Bengal.[17] The pricing barrier seemed to lessen somewhat with the agreement of the three states in July 2007 on at least part of the pricing formula.[18] But Tehran's abrupt dismissal on August 12, 2007, of Oil Minister Kazem Vaziri Hamaneh seemed to have raised this barrier still higher. According to news media accounts, the action against Hamaneh, a leading architect of the IPI pipeline's arduously negotiated tri-nation framework agreement, was taken ostensibly on grounds that he had offered to sell gas to India and Pakistan at an unacceptably high 30 percent discount. Rumored Iranian anger over Pakistan's alleged support for American clandestine activity in Iranian Balochistan was also said to be a possible factor. There was inevitably speculation that the pipeline project, which the Iranians had recently been claiming could begin to supply gas as early as 2011, had exited along with the Oil Minister.[19]

These already formidable obstacles have been given substantial reinforcement by Washington's stiff public opposition to the project and its threats to enforce sanctions against Iran.[20] Conveyed repeatedly and over several years to both Pakistan and India, the

Bush administration's distaste for Iranian ambitions in the region, including its alleged nuclear arms program, is extremely difficult for either country to ignore. Pakistan, anointed by Washington in March 2004 as a "major non-NATO ally," is the recipient of billions in American aid for its cooperation in the war against terrorism. India, in turn, is reluctant to put at risk the critically important civilian nuclear accord signed by the United States and India in July 2005. The accord took a major step towards implementation in July 2007 when the two governments reportedly reached agreement on the specific terms governing New Delhi's access to U.S. nuclear fuel and equipment.[21] Nevertheless, the deal has yet to be finally approved by the currently contumacious U.S. Congress. To ensure against India's backsliding on the pipeline matter, Washington dispatched Energy Secretary Samuel Bodman to India in March 2007 with the stern message, publicly delivered, that the IPI pipeline, if allowed to go forward, would "contribute to the development of nuclear weapons." And that, he made clear, had to be stopped.[22]

Added to all of these obstacles is the deep distrust that many Indians harbor when it comes to dealing with Pakistan on a matter as critical as India's energy security. No doubt, this basic distrust is aggravated by Pakistan's current domestic instability, including the potential for an out-of-control Baloch nationalist insurgency in Pakistan's sprawling province of Balochistan. The IPI pipeline, unavoidably vulnerable to acts of sabotage, would have to transit about 760 kilometers of "sensitive distance" (about 28 percent of the pipeline's total length) in this province.[23] Electronic monitoring of the pipeline can reduce the hazard; and repairs to damaged pipelines typically take from only a few hours to a few days.[24] According to most observers, however, gas pipelines of the proposed length are an easy target and difficult to defend; and attacks on them can have cumulatively severe economic costs. Baloch militants, as noted earlier, have taken increasingly in recent years to attacks on energy infrastructure. That development, even when the damage inflicted is minor, is bound to dampen investor confidence in energy ventures — a hugely important objective of Pakistan's economic strategists.[25]

As for the quadrilateral, America-boosted TAPI pipeline project, the obstacles are conceivably much worse. Setting aside the inevitable difficulties that arise in any four-party negotiation of this sort, the fact is that two of these parties (Afghanistan, Pakistan) present a security challenge — an estimated "sensitive transit distance," according to one source, of 1,200 kilometers, or 58 percent of the pipeline's length — that to most onlookers looks virtually insuperable.[26] Indeed, the full-blown insurgency that presently engulfs large parts of southern Afghanistan, on top of the frequent episodes of militant protest and violence in Pakistan's Balochistan, would appear for the time being to render entirely moot the issue of constructing the TAPI natural gas pipeline. That Washington has made clear its preference that New Delhi should scrap the IPI project and embrace the TAPI alternative does not necessarily add to its attraction for Indians. They, after all, might be at least as unwilling to place their country's energy security in American hands, which the TAPI pipeline — transiting U.S.-dominated Afghanistan — requires, as in Pakistan's. Admittedly, the Pakistan government's surprise announcement on August 20, 2007, that it had awarded a $10 billion contract to the American-based International Oil Company to build an oil and gas pipeline from Turkmenistan to Pakistan (TAP), extending all the way to Gwadar on the Balochistan coast, has breathed at least some life back into this pipeline option, albeit without India's explicit inclusion. But the TAP/TAPI project has been periodically "revived" over the past decade without material consequence, and the government's promise that the newly unveiled venture was scheduled for completion within 3 years falls noticeably short of credibility.[27]

The dim prospects for realization of these gas pipeline projects, especially in the near term, would appear certain to have some negative consequences for Balochistan and Baloch nationalism. For one, any material gains to development-starved Balochistan province that might have resulted from its being on the pipeline's path would be lost. Such gains include an opportunity for construction and maintenance jobs, for instance, or the possibility of a provincial share in gas transit fees, or wider distribution of natural gas within the province. Another negative is that the attention paid by the sensation-seeking news media to the militants' frequent resort to acts of sabotage against Balochistan's existing energy infrastructure seems bound to assist the government in its effort to fix the militants in the public mind as pernicious agents of Pakistan's rapidly mounting energy crisis, a crisis whose demonstrably adverse impact on the daily lives of most Pakistanis grows larger with each passing day.[28]

Pakistan's energy shortage is certain to shorten tempers, in other words, along with reducing ethnic tolerance. It does not matter that the militants' tactics for the most part have thus far inflicted only minor and quickly repaired damage—far less, one suspects, than the militants' capabilities would permit. What does count, however, is that these tactics, instead of winning converts to the Baloch cause, reinforce the government-promoted stereotype of the Baloch as reactionary, vengeful, and self-defeating foes of Pakistan's economic progress and of modernity itself.

Energy Geopolitics III: Gwadar and the Central Asia Transport Corridor.

In place of the ill-starred eastward-running natural gas pipelines, the region is witnessing instead the fast-paced development of competitive and politically divisive "transport corridors" built on a north-south axis. These corridors consist mainly of port, road, rail, and air infrastructural networks. The primary function of these networks is, along with promotion of commercial and political ties, to improve Indian or, as the case may be, Pakistani access to the energy-rich CARs and to achieve some influence over the production, processing, and distribution of energy resources. The inauguration on March 20, 2007, of Pakistan's Chinese-assisted Gwadar deep sea port on the Balochistan coast gave clear sign of Islamabad's intention for Pakistan to become the CARs' favored commercial and energy intermediary. The expected completion by the end of 2008 of the Indian-constructed Zaranj-Delaram highway in southwestern Afghanistan will give an equally transparent sign of New Delhi's similar intent.

President Musharraf inaugurated the Gwadar deep sea port in the presence of Chinese Minister for Communication Li Shen. Musharraf paid tribute in his address to the friendship between China and Pakistan that had made the port a reality. He dwelt at some length on the new seaport's potential for opening a major trade corridor to Central Asia, China, and

Turkmenistan. Included in the address was a blunt warning to "extremist elements" in Balochistan who would be "wiped out of this area" if they failed to surrender their weapons.[29]

Musharraf's comments at Gwadar, brief and inelegant as they were, commemorated an event of far more than passing interest to the countries in the region. An obscure fishing village with a population of about 5,000 when the project was begun in earnest in 2001, Gwadar has already grown into a bustling town of at least 125,000 — with prospects, if the current boom in real estate investment is any sign, of far greater expansion. Its location 650 kilometers (about 400 miles) west of Karachi provides some needed strategic depth for Pakistan's modest-sized naval force, subject in the past to the blockade of its major base at Karachi by the much more powerful Indian navy. However, the obvious military advantages gained by Pakistan from the new port are only one dimension of Gwadar's significance.

Interviewed by the author in March 2007, an official of Pakistan's Ministry of Ports and Shipping asserted with apparent confidence that Gwadar would within a few years rank among the world's biggest, best, and busiest deep sea ports. It had at the time of the inaugural event three functional berths, with space for at least 14 more. It had enormous advantages, the official claimed, over its rivals in the region, including Iran's port of Chabahar (see Map 1), located in the provinces of Balochstan and Sistan near the Pakistan border on the coast of the Gulf of Oman. Like Chabahar, the official insisted, Gwadar lies on major maritime shipping lanes close to the region's vast oil and gas resources, and also close to the rapidly growing and dynamic Persian Gulf economies. In contrast to Chabahar, however, Gwadar, he averred, is an all-year, all-weather, deep channel port that will eventually be able to offer accommodations for the largest oil tankers, along with ease of access to the docking area and unusually short turn-around times.[30]

Pakistani plans for Gwadar envision its evolution into a major multidimensional hub of economic activity, to be linked in coming years to a rapidly expanded web of road, rail, air, and pipeline networks to neighboring states, and potentially satellited by a liquid natural gas (LNG) terminal, a steel mill, an automobile assembly plant, a cement plant, and facilities for oil refining. Plans also call for a first-rate international airport at Gwadar.

Undoubtedly, it was "the convergence of Sino-Pakistani strategic interests [that] put the port project onto a fast track to its early completion";[31] and it is the Chinese connection with Gwadar, of course, that has attracted most attention from regional security observers. As the principal contributor (of about $200 million) to the project's first phase, China has transparent interests both in monitoring the supply routes for its rapidly increasing energy shipments from the Persian Gulf and also in opening an alternative route via Pakistan for import/export trade serving China's vast, sometimes restive, and rapidly developing Muslim-majority Xinjiang Autonomous Region.

From New Delhi's point of view, the strategic implications of the Gwadar project are substantial — and clearly worrisome. First, Gwadar complicates the Indian navy's strategic planning. It is one of several naval bases mentioned by Musharraf in his inaugural comments, two of them on the Balochistan coast, which Pakistan is building to diversify and deepen its naval defenses. It is one of several signs that Pakistan aspires to a significantly greater and better-defended naval presence in the Indian Ocean.

Second, the construction of Gwadar and its associated road, rail, and pipeline networks has been openly justified as a means to materially strengthen Pakistan's influence with Afghanistan and the Central Asian states, with whom it is already formally associated in the Economic Cooperation Organization founded by Turkey, Pakistan, and Iran in 1985 and expanded to its present membership of 10 (entirely Muslim states) in 1992.

Third, New Delhi will inevitably view Gwadar as another link in the China-built chain encircling India on its eastern, northern, and western borders. More perhaps than any other development in the history of Sino-Pakistan relations, Gwadar extablishes the major infrastructural framework for substantially strengthened military and economic ties between Pakistan and China. Potentially, these ties could lead to Pakistan's near absorption into a China-centric strategic partnership.[32]

Last, but by no means least important, New Delhi now has to reckon as well with the strategic significance of Washington's own increasingly aggressive engineering activity in the region. On August 26, 2007, U.S. Secretary of Commerce Carlos Gutierrez presided over the dedication of a 673-meter long bridge over the Pyanj River dividing Tajikistan and Afghanistan. The bridge, costing over $37 million and able to handle as many as 1,000 trucks per day, is the largest U.S. Government-funded infrastructure project in Tajikistan. Described by the Commerce Secretary as a "physical and symbolic link between Central Asia and South Asia,"[33] the bridge is a transparent challenge to Russia's continued dominance in the Central Asian region. Indians could not help noticing, however, that U.S. Embassy press releases at the time called attention (not without some irony) to *Karachi* as a "warm water port" and to *Pakistan* as the southern destination of the bridge's future traffic.[34]

New Delhi is, of course, not without its own plans for developing energy-motivated transport corridors reaching into CARs. Formally launched in 2000, the International North-South Transport Corridor (INSTC) was a first step in this direction. It joined India initially with Russia and Iran, and eventually with several other Asian and European nations, in a project meant primarily to draw Europe-bound commercial trade traffic away from the Suez Canal to an alternative and much shorter road, rail, and sea route leading from the major Iranian port of Bandar Abbas northwestward to the Caspian Sea and beyond to the St. Petersburg gateway and Europe. A branch of INSTC led into Turkmenistan.

When the Taliban regime was driven from Kabul in November 2001, the way was cleared for a still more ambitious Indo-Iranian plan calling for the addition of a second INSTC route in Iran's less populated eastern sector. One of the first items on New Delhi's list of aid projects for the new Northern Alliance-based government in Afghanistan was construction of a 218-kilometer (135-mile) Zaranj-Delaram highway link reaching from the Iranian border in southwestern Afghanistan to Afghanistan's existing intercity ring road (Map 2, left-hand arrow), from there to Feyzabad, and thence to Tajikistan in Central Asia (Map 2, right-hand arrow). The new highway was intended to connect with Iranian roads (and, eventually, with a new rail line) leading to Iran's port of Chabahar (Map 1) currently under development with Indian assistance. The project was publicized as providing Afghanistan with a route to the sea shorter than was currently available through

Pakistan. The need to bypass Pakistan, which had consistently stonewalled Indian requests for overland commercial access to Afghanistan and Central Asia, partially drove New Delhi's plan.[35] This plan naturally creates anxiety in Islamabad, which cannot at this point be certain of the success of its own Gwadar scheme (see Map 1).

Map 2. Zaranj-Delaram Highway Link from Iran, across Afghanistan, to Tajikistan.

Baloch nationalism thus finds itself astride two nearby and rival transport corridors under construction, with the region's economic future at stake in their success or failure. Moreover, the Baloch tribal minority's relentlessly-voiced demands for equity, justice, and self-determination again confront the powerful drivers of energy security, with intensified urgency and ever higher stakes. That the Baloch are positioned to be a major beneficiary of this development — as well as to be a major actor, negative or positive, on its prospects —

is abundantly clear. It is just as clear, however, that Islamabad's design—as implied in Musharraf's inaugural comments at Gwadar—has thus far mainly been to sweep them aside, apparently reflecting the view that this option is simpler and presents fewer risks.

Baloch Nationalism: Aims and Potential.

The Baloch nationalist movement is not a unitary force. Neither in its leadership nor in its tactics and goals does it speak with one voice. For some Baloch nationalists, the horizon of nationalism does not extend much beyond the boundary of a single tribal identity— Marri or Bugti, for instance. For others, the horizon embraces all of the 70-odd Baloch tribes resident within or near the borders of Balochistan. Some Baloch nationalists demand complete independence. Most, hailing the 1973 Constitution as a workable basis for a reconstructed and strengthened federalism, limit their aspirations to greater autonomy. Anti-state violence has been the chosen tactic of some. For the great majority, a remedy of grievances has been sought mainly through established state institutions. Notwithstanding these differences, however, there is virtually no chance that the problems confronting Islamabad arising from the current resurgence of Baloch nationalism can be swept aside.

The actual scale of the present Baloch rebellion is a matter of considerable controversy, not only with regard to the number of tribesmen under arms but also to the number of tribes directly involved, the amount of damage they have inflicted, and their degree of success in maintaining control over significant swaths of provincial territory. Fueling the controversy is the fact that much of Balochistan is inaccessible and off limits to news media representatives and independent observers. That has made reliable and verified information about the fighting there extremely hard to come by. There are huge differences, for instance, in the estimates given of the number of tribesmen currently in rebellion. One close observer has claimed that the Bugti tribe alone has as many as 10,000 tribesmen under arms.[36] A leading English-language newspaper in Islamabad, *The Nation*, quoted President Musharraf as having told a gathering of Pakistan Muslim League-Quaid-i-Azam(PML-Q) leaders on March 26, 2005, that the Bugti, Marri, and Mengal tribal chiefs commanded private armies of 7,000, 9,000, and 10,000 men, respectively.[37] Spokesmen for the Pakistan army interviewed by the author in early 2007 ridiculed such figures, insisting instead that to label the sporadic and often desultory acts of violence as an insurgency was itself fundamentally misleading.

A senior police bureaucrat in an off-the-record interview with the author at the same time put the figure of full-time fighters for the *entire* insurgency at no more than 1,000.[38] According to him, the Baloch militants are "not a structured army or organization." The so-called Balochistan Liberation Army (BLA) and Balochistan Liberation Force (BLF), he said, are "myths [existing] only on paper." In fact, he claimed, only two tribes, the Marris and the Bugtis, are responsible for most of the violence; and only one of them, the Marris, is a major problem. The third of the trio of historically troublesome tribes, the Mengals, have few tribesmen under arms, he added, and generally offer little but moral encouragement to the militants. This means that the insurgency, in this official's view, is a serious law-

and-order problem in only two of the province's 27 districts, and only a minor vexation elsewhere.

The government's estimates of the rebels' man-power have waxed and waned over time depending on circumstances and the government's immediate political desire either to over- or understate the problem's magnitude. Minimizing the number of rebels suits Islamabad's present understandable objective to have Balochistan seen by potential foreign investors in the mega-projects discussed above as a good place to invest. But such a picture is almost certainly excessively sanguine. Many well-positioned and knowledgeable individuals among the author's interlocutors, while freely admitting the relative narrowness of the insurgency's immediate tribal and territorial base, insisted that severe alienation from the Pakistan state was spreading rapidly to the province's urban areas and to growing numbers of educated Baloch youths. That trend, unless reversed, would, of course, give the nationalist movement an entirely different and much more threatening coloration. Given the fairly massive scale achieved by the 1970s insurrection, Islamabad is in no position to be complacent over the present rebellion's currently more limited dimensions.

Baloch nationalism has deep roots in Pakistan. In fact, alienation from the state has been a constant in Pakistan's post-independence history ever since 1948 when the country's fledgling military, faced with an independence movement in Kalat in southern Balochistan, forceably annexed the principality. In the years since, indigenous alienation has from time to time led to renewed rebellion, as in the 1970s with the eruption of a full-scale insurgency so well described in the pages of Selig Harrison's book. While no Baloch rebellion has extended to the entire province or succeeded in mobilizing more than a handful of the Baloch tribes that dwell there, distrust of the Punjab-dominated central government and festering discontent with the political order fostered over the years by that government are very widely shared among the Baloch. They constitute a nearly inexhaustible source of fuel for the nationalist agenda.[39]

There is, in fact, powerful evidence that Balochistan has not fared well at all in Pakistan's political order. For instance, a recent and methodologically sophisticated study that disaggregated Pakistan's gross domestic product (GDP) into its provincial components for the years 1972-73 to 1999-2000—a period of 28 years—found that the Punjab alone of the country's four provinces had seen its share of national GDP rise. The North West Frontier Province (NWFP) had managed merely to maintain its share while Sindh and Balochistan provinces saw theirs reduced by about 1 percentage point each—in Balochistan's case falling from 4.5 to 3.7 percent. The figures looked even more dismal, moreover, when broken out in terms of per capita GDP. In the Punjab, per capita GDP rose annually in the period surveyed by about 2.4 percent, in the NWFP by 2.2 percent, in Sindh (even with the country's industrial colossus of Karachi included) by only 1.7 percent, and in Balochistan by a miserable 0.2 percent. "The results," observed study authors Kaiser Bengali and Mahpara Sadaqat, "tend to confirm earlier evidence of an emerging north-south economic divide in the country." They also concluded, somewhat despairingly, that "on the whole, Balochistan appears—at best—to remain trapped in a low-level equilibrium and—at worst—regressing further into under-development."[40]

Baloch leaders have been arguing for years that turning the situation around required, among other things, an overhaul of the rules governing intergovernmental fiscal relations — including both those pertaining to how the central government shares the divisible pool of tax revenues with the provinces (the so-called "vertical" distribution), and those pertaining to how the provincial share is divided up among the four provinces (the so-called "horizontal" distribution). There is apparent agreement among the provinces that the provincial share in the vertical distribution, now set at 47.5 percent of revenue collected, should be set at 50 percent.

However, where the Baloch are most adamant about the need for change, and where there is as yet no consensus among the provinces, is in the area of horizontal distribution. As it now stands, revenues are distributed among the provinces in accord with a strict per capita population criterion. This formula finds favor in the Punjab, and to some extent also in Sindh and the NWFP. It means, of course, that Balochistan, with just short of 5 percent of the country's population, inevitably gets a very small share of the pie. Possessing, on the other hand, 43.6 percent of the country's area, with the unique costs entailed thereby, along with an exceptionally low level of development, Balochistan, say its advocates, requires a different distributional formula.

One such formula, proposed by the renowned economist Mahbub ul Haq, would adjust the provincial population weight in accord with a complicated formula involving a number of factors — the income level of each province, the disparity of physical infrastructure and social services, and differences in fiscal discipline and revenue-generating effort.[41] Another approach offers an Inverse Population Density (IPD) formula, in which the size of the province is given due weight.[42] All such formulas are premised on the reasonable conviction that population, while obviously the simplest criterion, is "not always a reasonable approximation of need," and that Pakistan should not remain wedded to a conflict-generating criterion that has long since been abandoned by other countries, including India.[43]

Obviously, not all Baloch grievances can be as readily addressed as by adoption of an alternative revenue distribution formula. Baloch leaders have for many years claimed, in particular, that they are being demographically displaced and marginalized in their own province, the reasons for which will be discussed below. While reliable population figures in regard to Balochistan's ethno-linguistic composition are notoriously hard to come by, demographic circumstances and trends in the province lend this claim strong support. Pakistan's fifth and most recent national census taken in 1998 reported a total national population of 132.3 million. Of that, Balochi-speakers accounted for 3.57 percent, or around 4.72 million. Roughly 3.59 million of these Balochi-speakers (2.71 percent of the national population) resided in Balochistan. The population of Balochistan province itself was given as 6.5 million (4.96 percent of the national population). Baloch (including the Brahui dialect), the language of the province's titular ethnicity, was given as the mother tongue of 54.7 percent of the provincial population; Pashtu, the language of the second largest group, the Pashtuns, of about 29.6 percent.[44]

Language data from the 1972 census were never published; and in the census taken in 1981, language data were collected on a household rather than individual basis, frustrating intercensus and intergroup comparisons. The 1998 figures themselves,

26

in any event, are not taken as fully authoritative, even in official quarters. For instance, in a briefing in 2005 given by the Home Secretary of Balochistan to members of the Parliamentary Committee on Balochistan, the province's ethnic composition was said to be 45 percent Baloch and 38 percent Pashtun.[45]

Two important facts should be kept in mind with regard to Baloch demography. One is that many Pakistani Baloch, 23.9 percent of the total if we extrapolate from the figures above, live outside of Balochistan, especially in Sindh. The second is that the Baloch may already be a minority in Balochistan, and, even if one chooses to accept the official census figures, they are almost certainly heading in that direction. One reason for this is that more than a quarter-century of nearly continuous warfare in neighboring Afghanistan has resulted in the influx into Balochistan's northern districts of hundreds of thousands of Afghan refugees, most of them Pashtuns. Many of them are expected to remain there, substantially augmenting the province's already formidable Pashtun minority. Another reason is that the development of Gwadar is almost certain to result eventually in a huge influx — estimates run as high as 5 million — of non-Baloch into the province's southern reaches. Sandwiched as they are between these two seemingly inexorable immigrations, the Baloch have good cause for worry.

The fact is that modernization, globalization, Pakistan's steadily rising population, and the massive forces of change unleashed by economic development are threatening to leave the Baloch far behind. They are among the poorest, least educated, and least urbanized of Pakistan's population; and they are too easily passed over or pushed aside in the highly competitive social and economic environments now gaining traction in Pakistan. This is in part, of course, a structural problem, not lending itself readily to policy manipulation. But these circumstances did not arise unassisted by the government, whose policies have almost never been designed to give serious attention to Baloch problems.

One final facet of Balochistan's contemporary situation impacting heavily on the aims and potential of Baloch nationalism is best described as the military-strategic environment encircling the province. By this, I mean that the present insurgency is taking place amid circumstances that, by any reckoning, merit classification as among the most unstable, violent, and turbulent on the planet. In neighboring Afghanistan, there is a bloody war in progress involving the armed forces of many nations, with no end in sight. The spill-over effects into Balochistan — in the form, for instance, of the province's harboring of fugitives from the fighting or its provision of sanctuary or training camps for forces hostile to the U.S.-led coalition forces[46] — have already turned Balochistan into something akin to a second front in the Afghanistan war. On August 12, 2007, Pakistan's President Musharraf made the surprising admission at a major tribal gathering in Kabul that Afghan militants were indeed getting support from Pakistani soil.[47]

Observers often name the provincial capital, Quetta, as the chief haunt of al-Qaeda and Neo-Taliban chieftans. Pakistan routinely accuses India of using its consulates in both Afghanistan and Iran for the dispatch of covert agents in aid of the Baloch rebels.[48] Speculation is rife about which "foreign hand" is currently most busily engaged in Balochistan in the dirty business of arms supply, espionage, sabotage, and assassination. In regard to the assassination of Chinese engineers in Balochistan, in particular, responsibility has been variously assigned, in addition to the Baloch militants, to a grand assortment of agents, including the "Uighurs from the Uighur diaspora in Pakistan,"[49] and the governments of India, Iran, Afghanistan, the United Arab Emirates, Russia, and even the United States. One conspiracy-obsessed published narrative, blithely passing over a host of contradictions, offered the unlikely thesis that Baloch nationalism's most potent international support was coming from a U.S.-Russia-India intelligence triad whose diverse motives somehow converged in Balochistan![50]

While the larger part of this speculation about foreign covert activities in Balochistan must be taken with more than a pinch of salt, the ample record of such activities in this part of the globe merits serious attention. Pakistan has plenty of antagonists in the region; and the Baloch insurgency, after all, can readily serve more ends than those of the Baloch themselves.

Pakistan's Response to Baloch Nationalism.

Reliable information about the fighting in Balochistan has always been scarce; and in Pakistan's perennially overheated political environment, disinformation flourishes and propaganda frequently masquerades as objective fact. Even experienced commentators may from time to time fall victim to one side or the other's deliberately disseminated disinformation.[51] It is essential, therefore, to treat carefully the subject of Pakistan's counterinsurgency strategy. Nevertheless, the allegations hurled at the security forces — of indiscriminate killing of noncombatants, collective reprisals, coercive disappearances, and arbitrary arrests, all against a background of wanton disregard of civil rights and legal protections enshrined in the country's generally unheeded constitution — are simply too numerous and too convincingly documented to be lightly dismissed.[52] To be sure, at times in this conflict unfettered brutality appears to have been the rule of engagement on all sides. The markedly superior numbers and firepower of the government's forces make it virtually certain, however, that the lapses occur far more often, and with far worse consequences, at their hands. What, then, can confidently be said of Pakistan's so-called "strategy of conflict management"? In particular, how has it impinged on Pakistan's energy planning vis-à-vis tribal nationalist unrest in Balochistan?[53]

First of all, the impression is inescapable that Islamabad, in the words of a 2006 International Crisis Group (ICG) report, "pins its hopes on a military solution",[54] it has, in other words, placed its faith overwhelmingly in the multifaceted and forceful suppression of the Baloch nationalist movement. This is consistent with the counterinsurgent strategy the government employed under the civilian leadership of Zulfikar Ali Bhutto in the 1970s. In some respects, however, the current version of counterinsurgency — in its single-mindedness, inflexibility, and comprehensiveness — far surpasses the admittedly brutal approach the government took toward the tribal uprising in the 1970s. In this regard, Selig Harrison's recent assessment — that the Musharraf government "is using new methods, more repressive than those of his predecessors, to crush the insurgency"[55] — is certainly correct. What accounts for this, I believe, are the added pressures of energy security in the mix of factors driving the government's strategy of conflict management in Balochistan. Nothing else explains as well Islamabad's apparent endorsement of what is, in the last analysis, a virtually "zero-tolerance" model.

This model has three main elements, the first two of which are mainly carryovers from the 1970s insurgency:

1. **Information management: psychological warfare, information operations, and public diplomacy**. One important element of the strategy falls under the heading of what is nowadays commonly designated as "psychological warfare," or "information operations," or, especially when directed at foreign audiences, "public diplomacy." Though extremely difficult to measure, some of the themes that have been emphasized by the government in programs of this sort have very likely had the desired impact on target audiences, especially in the West. One such theme, elaborated by spokesmen for the Pakistan army in discussions with the author in early 2007, was that the "real" problem in Balochistan was the persistence of the backward and anachronistic *sardari* or *tumandari* system—in which ordinary Baloch occupied social positions distinctly inferior to those of the tribal leaders, the sardars or tumandars. These tribal chiefs and subchiefs, it is claimed, lord it over ordinary tribesmen, treating them virtually as bonded labor, demanding total submission and loyalty, and, to enforce conformity, meting out severe punishments including incarceration in tribal prisons or even death.[56]

From the army's perspective, the so-called insurgency is little more than the dying gasp of an obsolete and terribly oppressive system of tribal authority. It has very little to do, as the army describes it, with Baloch self-determination or Baloch defense against *government* oppression, and much to do instead with defending an oppressive system of *traditional tribal authority*—with perpetuating, in other words, the power and privilege of traditional tribal elites. In this telling, the sardars fear that modernity—in the form of government-sponsored roads, schools, electricity, health clinics, improved water supply, democratic institutions, and so on—will eventually erode their authority. They fight back by mobilizing and arming tribal militias against alleged government "encroachment" on tribal terrain and also against alleged "expropriation" of natural resources properly belonging to the indigenous tribes.[57]

Apart from methodically blaming and disparaging the tribal leadership, the government's information initiative has included belittlement of the insurgency's scale. This has been done in terms not only of the number of fighters in rebellion mentioned earlier, but also in terms that emphasize the absence of genuine ideological motivation among the insurgents as well as the extraordinary narrowness of their tribal base. Most of what is written about the militancy problem in Balochistan, an army spokesman heatedly assured me, is concocted: "It is *not* an insurgency. . . . The Baloch militants are *employed* people [mercenaries]. There is no [nationalist or other ideological] motivation!"[58] Only three of over 70 tribes, he said, account for the bulk of the insurgents—the Bugtis, Mengals, and Marris. Concentrated mainly in only three (Dera Bugti, Kohlu, and Khuzdar) of the province's 27 districts, they have very little support from the rest of the Baloch tribes; and even these three tribes, he assured me, are highly fractionalized, with most of the tribesmen, in fact, favoring the government side.

In sum, the government's information management strategy aims at belittlement and disparagement of the Baloch political leadership. The unfortunate effect is to depict the objectives of its Baloch adversaries in terms that discourage and delegitimize political compromise and accommodation, while at the same time providing justification for the government's determination to employ whatever methods are required, however unsavory, to crush the nationalist movement once and for all.

2. **Political management: political harassment and intimidation; decapitation of separatist leadership; divide and rule; and co-option of tribal leadership**. Government and Baloch statements explaining the reasons for the government's crackdown on Baloch nationalist political leadership naturally differ; but that a determined crackdown has been in progress for the past 3 years or so is openly acknowledged. Excellent accounts exist of the government's actions in this vein,[59] and there is no need to repeat all the details here. In general, these actions consist of mass arrests of Baloch political activists, numbering, in most accounts, in the many hundreds or even thousands; exploitation of the many fissures found within the Baloch ethnicity itself, both between the major tribal groups and within them; and the encouragement of divisions and distrust between the province's two largest ethno-national groupings—the Pashtuns and the Baloch. Differing ethno-linguistically and mobilized into separate political parties, these two groupings inevitably compete for political space in the province. In their rivalry lies ample opportunity for government interference and manipulation.

In early February 2003 when the Baloch insurgency was still at a relatively low boil, President Musharraf appointed retired former corps commander Lieutenant General Abdul Qadir Baloch to the crucial provincial post of governor. Reasons given for his dismissal from that post barely 6 months later in early August 2003 have included alleged corruption and, according to an official source, "that he hailed from the relatively small Zehri tribe in Balochistan and [therefore] could not play his role effectively, keeping in view the dominant influence of the much stronger sardars of other major tribes."[60] Another account—unverified—told to the author in an off-the-record interview in Islamabad in early 2007 by a senior political notable, was that General Abdul Qadir infuriated Musharraf by attempting on his own initiative to negotiate an end to tribal disturbances at Dera Bugti with Nawab Akbar Khan Bugti. Earlier as Quetta corps commander, Qadir had already had some notable success in this regard.[61]

Reportedly, only two persons were considered as Qadir's replacement—Lieutenant General (retired) Ali Jan Orakzai, an Orakzai Pashtun,[62] and Owais Ahmad Ghani, a Kakar Pashtun with ancestral ties to Balochstan.[63] Owais Ghani got the nod. Ethnic ties and the possible willingness of a Pashtun leader at that time to go along with heavier reliance on military force to settle matters with the Baloch almost certainly would have figured in Musharraf's calculations. Interestingly, General Abdul Qadir, at one time spoken of as a loyal friend of Musharraf, quickly associated himself, following his removal, with other prominent Pakistanis in public efforts calling upon Musharraf to either resign as President or as Chief of Army Staff.[64]

Decapitation efforts also have a long history in the Balochistan struggle. Arrest, imprisonment, assassination, and involuntary exile of prominent Baloch leaders were features of Zulfikar Bhutto's approach to Balochistan as well. Three recent and highly publicized cases are especially notable in this regard. The first was the killing on August 26, 2006, of Nawab Akbar Khan Bugti at his cave hideout in Marri territory (Kohlu district). He was the influential leader of the Baloch nationalist Jamhoori Watan Party (Republican National Party). Culminating a massive siege by army special forces, the killing of the nearly 80-year old tribal leader along with

many of his associates removed from the scene a politically cunning and charismatic figure, whose death,
some believe, dealt "a major blow to the insurgency"
and gave Islamabad "a decisive edge over the Baloch
rebel movement."[65] Bugti, having been in earlier years
both Governor and Chief Minister of Balochistan and
having worked hand-in-glove with Zulfikar Bhutto
against the tribal insurgents in the 1970s, hardly fit the
stereotype of a tribal guerrilla fighter. In recent years,
however, he had emerged as one of the most irritating
thorns in Musharraf's side. Precisely how he perished
is controversial, with some government spokespersons
claiming that he died when the walls of the cave col-
lapsed on him during the fighting, but with the government's critics insisting that he was the intended victim
of a state-directed assassination.

The second case, following almost immediately in
the wake of Bugti's death, was that of Sardar Akhtar
Mengal, former Chief Minister of Balochistan and
head of the Balochistan National Party (BNP). Mengal
was the son of Ataullah Mengal, the aging sardar of
the Mengal tribe and one of the tribal icons of the 1970s
rebellion. Mengal was arrested in November 2006 and
tried in the Karachi Anti-Terrorism Court for treason,
a fabricated charge in the view of many observers. He
was subjected, according to the eyewitness report of
a Human Rights Commission of Pakistan (HRCP) observer, to humiliating confinement in the courtroom
during the trial in a cage-like structure that prevented
any contact with his attorney. Mengal's example presented a stark warning to other disgruntled Baloch
tribesmen of the price to be paid for resistance to state
authority.[66] Mengal was acquitted of the treason charges in early 2007, but he was still in prison in early 2008
on other charges.

The third notable case of decapitation came in late November 2007 with the reported slaying by Pakistani security forces of guerrilla commander Nawabzada Balach Marri, the youngest of six sons of Nawab Khair Baksh Marri, another of the most eminent nationalist leaders of the 1970s insurgency. The younger Marri, leader of the banned Baloch Liberation Army (BLA), had apparently fled to Afghanistan in the wake of Nawab Akbar Khan Bugti's death in August 2006. Details of Marri's killing were not announced, but the resulting widespread outbursts of rage among his tribal kinsmen testified to the gravity of the loss.[67]

As one of Pakistan's most senior and highly respected journalists put it,

> Anyone challenging the military's authority in a country presently being ruled by the chief of army staff General Musharraf should think many times before daring to do so. Bugti paid with his life for committing this mistake [of] picking up the gun to fight the armed forces. Akhtar Mengal has launched a verbal assault only on the military and his punishment is imprisonment for an uncertain period in tough prison conditions.[68]

3. **Military management: increased deployment of security forces; new cantonments, military roads, and other infrastructure; and reliance on military repression.** The greatest divergence in management strategy between the 1970s insurgency and today's insurgency exists in the military realm. Underway today are plans for bringing responsibility for Balochistan's security more fully than ever before under central control, for increasing exponentially the central government's capacity for surveillance and policing there, and also for increasing dramatically the presence and reach in the province of the country's regular security forces. Foremost of these plans are:

- Establishment of three new military cantonments in Balochistan to augment the two now in existence at Sibi and Quetta. One is to be established at Gwadar on the southern coast, another at Kohlu, where the rebellious Marri tribe is headquartered, and a third at Dera Bugti, site of both the rebellious Bugti tribal headquarters as well as of the huge Sui natural gas fields.
- Elimination by 2010 of the separate and indigenously-recruited tribal police forces (levies) presently responsible for policing the so-called Category B areas, nonurban portions constituting 95 percent of the provincial territory. These tribal police forces are to be integrated into the regular provincial police, which up to now bore responsibility only for urban provincial territory, the so-called Category A, amounting to 5 percent.[69]

The government's preoccupation nowadays with Pakistan's energy security assuredly looms large in these military management strategies—aimed obviously at increasing the central government's policing and surveillance capabilities. In the absence of their determined implementation, as the government understands the issue, none of the three crucial energy-related initiatives discussed earlier in this monograph—i.e., exploiting Balochistan's own as yet only partially tapped energy resources, laying natural gas pipelines transiting the province, and constructing the vast infrastructure for a transport corridor to Central Asia and Xinjiang—can be successfully accomplished. Much is at stake—Pakistan's economic progress, the security of its borders in a hostile neighborhood, and the future of its vital alliance relationships with China and the United States. Better, it is believed by the military leadership in Islamabad, to depend on coercive state power — the immediately at-hand and reliable security forces — than accede to the demands of a small, politically weak, recalcitrant, and untrustworthy ethno-tribal minority whose interests inevitably run significantly counter to those of the state.

It is not that accommodating the Baloch minority has not been thought about in the highest circles of government and military. On September 29, 2004, then Prime Minister Chaudhry Shujat Hussain announced the formation of a Parliamentary Committee on Balochstan, constituted to examine the situation in the province and to make recommendations to ameliorate conditions and promote inter-provincial harmony. The Committee produced an admirably detailed and comprehensive report at the end of 2005. Its recommendations, filling seven pages and numbering in the dozens, called for numerous programs and reforms including an increase in the provincial share of natural gas revenues, stricter implementation of the job quota for Balochistan-domiciled persons in the federal services, larger provincial representation on the Gwadar Port Authority, construction of new dams and reservoirs to counter drought conditions in the pro-vince, and the discontinuance of humiliating treatment of provincial citizens at hundreds of security check-points maintained by the federal government's Coast Guard and Frontier Corps personnel throughout the province.[70]

However, when it came to the exceedingly sensitive matter of new cantonments, the Committee took refuge in discreetly phrased language, urging delay in construction pending "resolution of major current issues of Balochistan, . . . so that the congenial atmosphere currently created may be sustained."[71] It was clear: the Committee members believed that construction of the new cantonments could not, and perhaps should not, be stopped.

Although the military-led government appeared willing, at least up until recent years, to give consideration to political options suggested by some members of the country's civilian political elite, genuine accommodation of the Baloch minority does not seem to have commanded the military's sincere and sustained interest. This fact was driven home forcefully to the author by comments made in a lengthy interview in January 2007 with a senior bureaucrat with years of top-level experience in Balochistan. He professed some sympathy with the viewpoint of the Baloch sardars. They routinely pointed out to him, he said, that government decisions in regard to planned mega-development projects in Balochistan, projects like the Gwadar deep sea port and the Kacchhi Canal irrigation project that would have a huge impact on the lives of Baloch, were taken without any participation at all by the Baloch. This, he said, was true. The projects were the product of a "military mindset," a "tunnel view" that precluded "carrying the people along" with government planning. This view, he added, was especially prominent among military intelligence officers. "If the Baloch sardars had been taken into confidence," he emphasized, "the militancy problem would have been diminished. . . . *Everything is possible if political dialogue is opened up, . . . even if the sardars are unreasonable.*"[72]

My interlocutor's willingness to parcel out the blame for the Baloch insurgency more widely than was customary for Pakistani government officials seemed to me a promising departure from the egregiously one-sided vilification campaigns characteristic of the "information operations" discussed above. Even more promising was his extraordinary confidence in the healing power of political dialogue. He did not strike me as naïve. On the contrary, he had dwelt at length during the interview on the subject of foreign support of the insurgents, arguing earnestly that a tiny handful of sardars could not possibly take on the government of Pakistan *unless* given material support from the outside. But even in the face of foreign interference, he averred, "all things are doable."

In this official's view, then, the government's methodical demonization of the offending sardars, even in cases where some amount of rebuke might have been warranted, has been counterproductive. The more they were hounded, harassed, and humiliated, the more certain the Baloch became that the government's real aim is to marginalize them and to reduce them to second class citizenship in their own province.

Observe that this official's endorsement of a distinctly *political* approach to the Baloch problem is not to be confused or conflated with the contention in some quarters (the recent ICG report, for instance) that "the conflict could be resolved easily," provided free and fair elections [were] held in Pakistan by the end of 2007.[73] That sort of sanguine claim relies much too heavily on hoped-for outcomes of "democratic transition" — in other words, changes in political attitudes and behavior expected from competitive elections, civilian-run legislative bodies, and accountability to voters — to bring the threatening tribal insurgency to a close. In this connection, it is well to keep in mind that the 1970s insurgency erupted in the midst of one of Pakistan's infrequent periods of civilian rule, with the country's leader—Zulfikar Ali Bhutto—displaying as little inclination to accommodate the Baloch leadership's quest for greater autonomy as today's military leadership. Pakistani democratization is not a magic carpet that will carry the country inexorably in the direction of better government.

The powerful geopolitical and geo-strategic forces we have been considering here—energy rivalry foremost among them—that today inhabit a regional environment involving India, China, Russia, Central Asia, Iran, and the United States, along with a host of substate entities like Balochistan, seem unlikely to yield a solution so easily. No doubt democratic elections are one essential component of a solution. But something more than an election—more than the mere substitution of civilian in place of military rule—is needed to right the obviously wrong circumstances facing Balochistan. That something more is meaningful recognition that Pakistan's energy security can be fully safeguarded only when Baloch nationalism has been accommodated in good faith. The Baloch need to become partners of energy development, not its enemies. Any other course is fraught with danger.

Conclusion.

To conclude, the context of today's Baloch separatist-motivated insurgency differs in important respects from that of its 1970s predecessor, most fundamentally in terms of energy resource developments in what some are calling the "Asian Middle East" (embracing parts of South, Central, and Southwest Asia). This change in the energy context exerts a powerful threefold impact on the insurgents' prospects—first, by lifting Balochistan and Baloch nationalism to a point much higher on the scale of central government priorities, warranting, as the government sees the problem, zero tolerance and a crushing response; second, by arming the Baloch insurgents both with greater incentives for reclaiming control of Balochistan and with the capacity to drive up the economic and political costs to the government of continuing insurgent activity; and third (on a more hopeful note), by creating major opportunities—specifically, by turning Balochistan into an important energy conduit in the region—to address Baloch nationalist demands in a positive and mutually acceptable manner. Despite the ruthlessness of the counterinsurgency strategy pursued by the government thus far, Balochistan's rapidly intensifying energy context could supply both the means and the incentives for bringing the insurgency to a swift, negotiated, and amicable end.

Persuading the Pakistan government to reverse course in Balochistan and engage the Baloch nationalists politically and with a far more measured and judicious resort to the military option, will not be easy. The problem is not the alleged military "mindset." The problem is rather more complicated. The energy-related and other strategic forces impacting on that part of the world join together in shaping Pakistani perceptions of their policy requirements, in some instances narrowing options, in others practically dictating Islamabad's actions. Unfortunately, as Justin Dunne has perceptively observed, these forces "have demanded that the central government more strongly exert its authority in Baluchistan."[74]

As in the 1970s, Balochistan still stands in the shadow of Afghanistan, a source of endless policy dilemmas for Islamabad; but innumerable other shadows, equally darkening and each with its own set of impera-tives, have emerged. Pakistan's energy imperatives relate not only to its own natural gas resources but also to the proposed importation of natural gas from Iran and/or Turkmenistan, as well as to its all-important collaboration with China in groundworking a north-south commercial and energy corridor. All these factors crowd in upon Pakistan's policymaking in regard to the circumstances in Balochistan. Particularly, every effort must be made to ensure that no more Chinese engineers are slain anywhere in Balochistan.[75] It seems highly unlikely that these imperatives will grow any less pressing as time goes on. Giving significantly higher priority to the accommodation of the Baloch tribal minority, in the face of these imperatives, will be a hard sell.

However, Islamabad must come to realize that ac-commodating the Baloch nationalists makes far better sense than either neglecting or exterminating them. After all, energy rivalry is not the only factor affecting the context of the Baloch insurgency. Contemporary insurgency more generally, as Steven Metz persuas-ively argues, is undergoing fundamental change in its strategic context, structure, and dynamics, so that it bears less and less resemblance to its forebears. This metamorphosis, he says, mandates that governments adopt "a very different way of thinking about (and undertaking) counterinsurgency." The real threat posed by insurgency, he observes, is the deleterious effects of sustained conflict. Political destabilization and a host of other damaging pathologies may be the consequence of attempts to destroy insurgents. "Protracted conflict," he declares, "not insurgent victory, is the threat."[76]

Thus Pakistan's leaders, along with the leaders of states supporting Pakistan, should undertake on an urgent basis a reexamination of their policies so as to avoid if possible protracted conflict in Balochistan. The best overall way to do this is to make the Baloch partners to energy development, not antagonists of it.

ENDNOTES

1. The tribe and province are commonly spelled either as Baluch and Baluchistan or Baloch and Balochistan. The latter spelling seems currently to be winning out in writings on the subject and thus has been adopted here.

2. Selig S. Harrison, *In the Shadow of Afghanistan: Baluch Nationalism and Soviet Temptations*, Washington, DC: Carnegie Endowment for International Peace, 1981, p. 1.

3. Words themselves are, of course, weapons in the discourse of political conflict. Hence, the word "insurgency" is used with care here to mean a serious level of organized, widespread, and persistent anti-state violence without implying that the current separatist rebellion in Balochistan has reached the level attained by its 1970s forerunner, or that it has necessarily outstripped the government's capacity to contain it. The current rebellion certainly qualifies at a minimum as a "low-intensity insurgency."

4. Ending an 8-year reign as military ruler and a 46-year military career, Musharraf stepped down as chief of the Pakistan army and took the oath as civilian president in late 2007.

5. Indian President A. P. J. Abdul Kalam, an engineer by training, observed in a speech on energy security in 2005 that "energy independence has to be our nation's first and highest priority." Quoted in "India's President Seeks Energy Security," *Tech Policy*, August 17, 2005, available at *www.techpolicy.typepad. com/tpp/2005/08/indias_presiden_1.html*, accessed September 9, 2007.

6. Harrison, p. 7. Emphasis added.

7. B. Raman, "Security of Chinese Nationals in Pakistan," *International Terrorism Monitor*, Vol. 266, South Asia Analysis Group Paper No. 2329, August 11, 2007, available at *www.saag. org/papers24/paper2329.html*, accessed August 13, 2007.

8. For statistics regarding and description of Pakistan's energy resources, see Energy Information Administration, *Country Analysis Brief: Pakistan*, last updated December 2006, available at *www.eia.doe.gov*.

9. Petroleum & Natural Resources Division, Ministry of Petroleum & Natural Resources, Government of Pakistan, "Sui Southern Gas Company Limited: Introduction," available at *www. pakistan.gov.pk/divisions/ContentInfo.jsp?DivID=49&cPath=768_775 &ContentID=4177*, accessed September 11, 2007.

10. Naveed Ahmad, "Trouble in Pakistan's Energy-Rich Balochistan," *ISN Security Watch*, January 30, 2006, available at *www.isn.ethz.ch/news/sw/details.cfm?ID=14606*, accessed August 11, 2007.

11. Tarique Niazi, "Baloch Insurgents Escalate Attacks in Pakistan," *ISN Security Watch*, May 24, 2006, available at *www.isn. ethz.ch/news*, accessed August 11, 2007.

12. International Crisis Group (ICG), *Pakistan: The Worsening Conflict in Balochstan*, Asia Report No. 119, ICG, Islamabad/ Brussels, September 14, 2006, p. 16, available at *www.crisisgroup. org/library/documents/asia/south_asia/119_pakistan_the_worsening_ conflict_in_Balochstan.pdf*, accessed September 11, 2007.

13. M. Ziauddin, "Accessing Fossil Fuels in Balochistan," *Dawn*, September 4, 2006; and Mehtab Haider, "Balochistan Seeks Increase in Royalty," *The Nation*, January 24, 2005. See also Mansoor Akbar Kundi, "Provincial Autonomy: A View from Balochistan," in Pervaiz Iqbal Cheema and Rashid Ahmad Khan, eds., *Problems and Politics of Federalism in Pakistan*, Islamabad: Islamabad Policy Research Institute, 2006, especially p. 43.

14. ICG, pp. 16-17.

15. This and the next section incorporate some material from the author's paper, "In India's Lengthening Shadow: The US-Pakistan Strategic Alliance & the War in Afghanistan," presented in London on July 19, 2007, to an international seminar on Pakistan: Its Neighbors & the West, sponsored by the Royal United Services Institution (RUSI) and the Public Policy Research Organization (PPRO).

16. India's rapidly spiraling energy crisis is outlined in the author's paper, "The Progress of Détente in India-Pakistan Relations: New Chapter or Strategic Charade?" presentation to an international symposium on Pakistan: International Relations & Security, sponsored by the Institute of South Asian Studies (ISAS), National University of Singapore, May 24-25, 2007.

17. On the other hand, the Indian government's recent sobering 10- to 20-fold reduction in the estimated amount of domestic natural gas reserves projected for the Krishna Godavari basin is also bound to cast a new light on New Delhi's calculations in the IPI negotiations. India's probable future gas deficit now seems larger than ever. Siddarth Srivastava, "India Eyes Military Favors for Myanmar Oil," *AsiaTimes Online*, July 19, 2007, available at *www.atimes.com/atimes/South_Asia/IG20Df01.html*, accessed September 6, 2007.

18. "IPI Gas Price Formula Agreed," *Asian Age*, July 16, 2007. The cost of gas delivered through the IPI pipeline would be based, according to the agreement, on the price of natural gas in Japan, which accounts for roughly half the world's natural gas consumption.

19. Siddharth Srivastava, "Exit Iran's Oil Minister and a Pipeline Too," *AsiaTimes Online*, August 17, 2007, available at *www.atimes.com/atimes/South_Asia/IH17Df01.html*, accessed September 6, 2007; Kimia Sanati, "Iran: An Oil Industry That Lost Its Head," *AsiaTimes Online*, September 5, 2007; *www.atimes.com/atimes/Middle_East/II05Ak03.html*, accessed September 6, 2007; and "Iranian Oil Minister Steps Down," *Japan Today*, August 13, 2007, available at *www.freerepublic.com/focus/f-news/1880252/posts*, accessed September 6, 2007. For an illuminating comment on the pricing issue, see Kaveh L. Afrasiabi, "A Blockage in the Peace Pipeline," *AsiaTimes Online*, July 9, 2007, available at *www.*

atimes.com/atimes/South_Asia/IG10Df01.html, accessed September 6, 2007.

20. As of late January 2007, no firms had been sanctioned under the Iran Sanctions Act (ISA) or its predecessor Iran-Libya Sanctions Act (ILSA). Congress, in extending the Act to 2011, strengthened some of its provisions, but at the same time left the Executive Branch with considerable leeway in applying them. Kenneth Katzman, "The Iran Sanctions Act, ISA," *CRS Report for Congress*, Order Code RS20871, Washington, DC: Congressional Research Service, January 25, 2007.

21. Maura Reynolds, "U.S., India Reach Nuclear Accord," *Los Angeles Times*, July 28, 2007.

22. "We Need to Stop Pipeline, Says Bodman," *The Hindu*, March 23, 2007, available at *www.hinduonnet.com*, accessed September 10, 2007. See also Paranjoy Guha Thakurta, "Iran-Pakistan-India Gas Pipeline in Trouble," *Counter Currents*, February 14, 2006, available at *www.countercurrents.org/india-thakurta140206.htm*, accessed September 10, 2007; and Paranjoy Guha Thakurta, "US Frown Turns Gas Pipeline Into Pipe Dream," *Inter Press Service News Agency*, March 22, 2007, available at *www.ipsnews.net*, accessed on September 10, 2007.

23. Vinish Kathuria, "Promise of Transborder Gas Pipelines," *The Hindu*, May 8, 2006, available at *www.hindu.com/biz/2006/05/08/stories/2006050800341600.htm*, accessed on September 29, 2007; and Gal Luft, "Iran-Pakistan-India Pipeline: The Baloch Wildcard," *Energy Security*, Institute for the Analysis of Global Security, January 12, 2005, available at *www.iags.org/n0115042.htm*, accessed on April 2, 2007.

24. "Tough, but Workable Options," *Tehelka.com*, July 28, 2007, available at *www.tehelka.com*, accessed on September 29, 2007.

25. See, for instance, John Daly, "The Baloch Insurgency and Its Threat to Pakistan's Energy Sector," *Terrorism Focus*, Vol. 3, No. 11, March 21, 2006, available at *www.jamestown.org/terrorism/news*, accessed September 10, 2007; Tarique Niazi, "Baloch Insurgents Escalate Attacks on Infrastructure," *Terrorism Focus*, Vol. 3, No. 20, May 23, 2006, available at *www.jamestown.org/terrorism/news*, accessed on August 4, 2007; and Luft.

26. Kathuria.

27. "Editorial: How Realistic Is TAP Gas Pipeline?" *Daily Times*, August 21, 2007, available from: *www.dailytimes.com. pk/print.asp?page=2007%5C08%5C21%5Cstory_21-8-2007_pg*, accessed September 8, 2007.

28. The scale of Pakistan's energy crisis is, from all accounts, formidable. On this, see Khaleeq Kiani, "Power Crisis to Deepen in Coming Years: 50pc Demand Rise in Two Years Likely," *Dawn*, January 8, 2007; and "Massive Gas Shortfall Forecast," *Dawn*, March 7, 2007.

29. "President Musharraf's Address at the Inauguration of Gwadar Deep Seaport," available from *www.presidentofpakistan. gov.pk/FilesSpeeches/Addresses*, accessed on April 2, 2007.

30. Interview by author in Islamabad in March 2007. Name withheld on request.

31. Tarique Niazi, "Gwadar: China's Naval Outpost on the Indian Ocean," *Association for Asian Research*, February 28, 2005; available at *www.asianresearch.org/articles/2528.html*, accessed on April 4, 2007.

32. For a recent comment on the expansion and consolidation of Sino-Pakistani bilateral cooperation in the area of defense, see Syed Fazl-e-Haider, "China Rises to Pakistan's Defense," *AsiaTimes Online*, July 11, 2007, available at *www.atimes.com/atimes/ South_Asia/IG11Df02.html*, accessed on September 10, 2007.

33. Quoted in M. K. Bhadrakumar, "Afghan Bridge Exposes Huge Divide," *AsiaTimes Online*, September 4, 2007, available at *www.atimes.com/atimes/printN.html*, accessed on September 29, 2007.

34. Embassy of the United States in Dushanbe, Tajikistan, *Press Release: Fact Sheet on Tajik-Afghan Nizhny Pyanj Bridge*, n.d., available at *www.dushanbe.usembassy.gov/bridge_fact_sheet.html*, accessed on September 15, 2007. According to the Fact Sheet, "the bridge will provide the region with inter-connectivity by cutting

the distance between Dushanbe and seaports almost in half. It also facilitates access to a warm water port in Karachi, Pakistan, for the countries to the north. This should spur increased trade and economic development throughout the region."

35. Pakistan does not, however, deny overland passage to India of Afghanistan goods.

36. Frederic Grare, "Pakistan: The Resurgence of Baluch Nationalism," *Carnegie Papers*, No. 65, Washington, DC: Carnegie Endowment for International Peace, January 2006, p. 8.

37. Quoted in B. Raman, "Baloch Shadow Over Wen Jiabao's Visit," *South Asia Analysis Group* Paper No. 1339, April 18, 2005, available at *www.saag.org/papers14/paper1339.html*, accessed on September 10, 2007.

38. Interview by author in Pakistan in January 2007. Identity withheld on request.

39. Harrison's book, cited earlier, provides an excellent overview of Baloch history as well as the evolution of Baloch nationalism. The most useful recent account of the background and development of the current Baloch insurgency is that of the ICG, cited above. It is now available in updated form: ICG, *Pakistan: The Forgotten Conflict in Balochistan*, Asia Briefing No. 69, Islamabad/Brussels, October 22, 2007, available at *www. crisisgroup.org/library/documents/asia/south_asia/69_pakistan_the_ forgotten_conflict_in_Balochstan.pdf*, accessed on January 10, 2008. Other recent and valuable sources are Rajshree Jetly, "Baluch Ethnicity and Nationalism, 1971-81," *Asian Ethnicity*, Vol. 5, No. 1, February 2004, pp. 7-26; and Justin S. Dunne, *Crisis in Baluchistan: A Historical Analysis of the Baluch Nationalist Movement in Pakistan*, thesis submitted in June 2006 to the Department of National Security Affairs, Naval Postgraduate School, Monterey, California, p. 68, available at *www.ccc.nps.navy.mil/research/theses/ dunne06.pdf*, accessed on July 20, 2007.

40. Kaiser Bengali and Mahpara Sadaqat, *Regional Accounts of Pakistan: Methodology and Estimates 1973-2000*, Karachi: Social Policy and Development Centre, 2006, pp. 74-75.

41. Cited in Pervez Tahir, "Problems and Politics of Fiscal Federalism in Pakistan," in Cheema and Khan, p. 75.

42. Senate of Pakistan, *Report of the Parliamentary Committee on Balochistan*, Report 7, Islamabad: Senate Foreign Relations Committee, November 2005, p. 84.

43. Tahir, p. 76.

44. Complete census data are available online at *www.statpak. gov.pk.*

45. Senate of Pakistan, p. 12.

46. Laura King, "Battles Raging in Remotest Pakistan," *Los Angeles Times*, August 13, 2007, p. 1.

47. Taimoor Shah and Carlotta Gall, "Afghan Rebels Find a Haven in Pakistan, Musharraf Says," *The New York Times*, August 12, 2007.

48. On this issue, see Scott Baldauf, "India-Pakistan Rivalry Reaches into Afghanistan," *The Christian Science Monitor*, September 12, 2003; "Afghanistan Asked to Clamp Down Indian Consulates Interference in Balochistan," *PakTribune*, February 21, 2006, available at *www.paktribune.com/news*, accessed on July 25, 2007; and M. H. Ahsan, "'RAW Is Training 600 Baluchis in Afghanistan': Mushahid Hussain," *Boloji.com*, July 2, 2007, available at *www.boloji.com/analysis2/0116.htm*, accessed on April 20, 2007.

49. B. Raman, "Gwadar: Balochs Blast Deal with Singapore Company," *South Asia Analysis Group* Paper No. 2127, February 8, 2007, available at *www.saag.org/papers22/paper2127.html*, accessed on April 12, 2007.

50. Tariq Saeedi *et al.*, "Pakistan: Unveiling the Mystery of Balochistan Insurgency," *IntelliBriefs*, March 1, 2005, available at *www.intellibriefs.blogspot.com*, accessed on July 10, 2007.

51. A case in point is the description veteran writer Selig Harrison gives of the methods Islamabad is currently employing

50

against its Baloch nationalist adversaries. A "slow-motion genocide," he writes in a recent article, is being inflicted on the Baloch. In August 2006, thousands of them were forced to flee their villages "to escape bombing and strafing by the U.S.-supplied F-16 fighter jets and *Cobra* helicopter gunships of the Pakistan air force, ..." Pakistan President Pervez Musharraf, he alleges, "is using new methods, more repressive than those of his predecessors, to crush the insurgency." Baloch spokesmen, he says, "have reported large-scale kidnappings and disappearances, charging that Pakistani forces have rounded up hundreds of Baloch youths on unspecified charges and taken them to unknown locations." Selig S. Harrison, "Pakistan's Baluch Insurgency," *Le Monde Diplomatique*, October 5, 2006, available at *www.mondediplo.com/2006/10/05Balochistan*, accessed on August 4, 2007. With most of Harrison's description, there is no need to quibble. Some of it, however, is unnecessarily provocative. For one thing, his use of the word "genocide," even if in slow motion, is unwarranted. And his mention of F-16 fighter jets presents a real problem. In his article, Harrison cites the Human Rights Commission of Pakistan as the source for the reported use of F-16s in recent fighting. A careful reading of that group's meticulously assembled report published in early 2006 reveals, however, that there is no mention of that aircraft anywhere in it. It does mention bombings and also strafing by gunship helicopters; but it leaves to the reader's judgment whether Pakistan would not have used for this militarily rather piddling task some of the hundreds of much cheaper Chinese-supplied fighter aircraft in its inventory as opposed to any of the dwindling stock of its very expensive, nuclear capable, aging but still highly prized F-16s. Similarly, the 2006 International Crisis Group report on Balochistan also states categorically that "U.S.-supplied *Cobra* helicopters and F-16s" are being used against the Baloch." ICG, *Pakistan: The Worsening Conflict in Balochistan*, p. 22, reference 180. The ICG report cites an article in *The New York Times* contributed by correspondent Carlotta Gall in support of its contention. Gall's sole cited source for this information, however, was an interview with Baloch nationalist leader Nawab Akbar Khan Bugti (at the time a guiding force of the Baloch insurgency and a shrewd but hardly impartial witness) who had told the American journalist, with perhaps the hope of bringing American pressure down upon Islamabad, "that the government was using its American-supplied jets and helicopter gunships against them." Carlotta Gall, "In Remote Pakistan Province, a Civil War Festers,"

The New York Times, April 2, 2006. Given the extraordinary strategic significance that has for decades been attached to America's sale of F-16s to Pakistan, any reference to their use against Pakistan's own citizens (especially when linked with the politically-charged reference to the "genocidal" onslaught of Pakistan's armed forces) is inevitably freighted with potentially serious political implications.

52. There are a number of revealing reports on human rights violations in Balochistan. For a report that emphasizes the government's transgressions, see Human Rights Commission of Pakistan (HRCP), *Conflict in Baluchistan: Human Rights Violations*, Report of Fact-Finding Missions December 2005-January 2006, Lahore: HRCP, 2006. For a report that catalogues abuses by both sides but that is weighted heavily against the Baloch tribal chiefs, see Ansar Burney Trust International, *HR Violations in Balochistan: 2005-2006*, Fact-Finding Report by ABTI, Karachi: ABTI, 2006.

53. The content of this section draws to a large extent on the author's interviews in recent years on the Baloch question with a fairly broad assortment of serving Pakistan military intelligence officers, retired senior bureaucrats with service in Balochistan, human rights investigators, senior police officials, professional analysts, veteran politicians, academics, and others. In most instances, they requested — and are granted — anonymity.

54. ICG, *The Worsening Conflict in Balochistan*, p. 22.

55. Harrison, "Pakistan's Baluch Insurgency."

56. The alleged sadistic cruelty of the sardars, especially of the powerful, recently-slain head of the Bugti tribe, Nawab Akbar Khan Bugti, looms as the principal theme in an obviously propagandistic, pro-government photo magazine published a few years ago showing, apart from gruesome photos of the sardar's torture victims, the huge arsenal of modern weaponry he had assembled with which to fight the government. *Terrorism in Balochistan & Government's Response*, Quetta, no date and no sponsorship identified.

57. Noticeable in the Pakistan government's depiction of the struggle over Balochistan is a striking continuity between the

themes currently in use and those used in earlier periods of armed confrontation. Propaganda cartoons distributed by the Zulfikar Bhutto government during the 1970s insurgency, for instance, played heavily on the oppressive tribal authority theme. One set of cartoons featured in that period, for instance, cleverly displayed a sword (in Arabic, *zulfikar*) happily evoking Bhutto's own name and wielded by Bhutto's People's Party government, slicing off the hand of the dreaded *sardari* system, thus freeing from bondage the suppressed Baloch held in its clutches. Sample cartoons are reprinted in the author's study, *The Baluchis and Pathans*, Report No. 48, London: Minority Rights Group, 1981.

58. Interview by the author in Rawalpindi in January 2007. Identity withheld on request.

59. See, for instance, ICG, *The Worsening Conflict in Balochistan*, pp. 19-25; HRCP, *Conflict in Baluchistan*; Grare, *Pakistan: The Resurgence of Baluch Nationalism*; and Rajshree Jetly, "The Re-emergence of the Baluch Movement in Pakistan," *ISAS Insights*, No. 15, Singapore: Institute of South Asian Studies, October 1, 2006.

60. Ismail Khan, "Owais Confirms His Nomination: Balochistan Governor," *Dawn*, August 9, 2003.

61. Syed Saleem Shahzad, "Balochistan Tribes Threaten Pakistan's Gas Riches," *AsiaTimes Online*, July 25, 2002, available at *www.atimes.com*, accessed on August 15, 2007.

62. In a development seeming to mirror the Pakistan government's increasing difficulties in managing insurgent activity in the country's northwest, Owais Ghani was shifted in early January 2008 to the post of NWFP governor, a position vacated, ironically, by the sudden resignation of Lieutenant General (retired) Ali Muhammad Jan Orakzai, who had been Ghani's main rival for posting as governor of Balochistan.

63. Shahzad, "Balochistan Tribes Threaten Pakistan's Gas Riches."

64. Praveen Swami, "Balochistan Shadow Over India-Pakistan Ties," *The Hindu*, May 9, 2006.

65. "Pakistan: The Death of a Rebel Leader," *Strategic Forecasting*, August 26, 2006, available at *www.stratfor.com*, accessed on April 20, 2007.

66. Malik Siraj Akbar, "Taking on the State," *Frontline*, Vol. 24, No. 4, February 24-March 9, 2007, available at *www.hinduonnet. com/fline*, accessed on April 15, 2007.

67. Saleem Shahid, "Balach Marri killed: Violence in Quetta, Schools Closed," *Dawn*, November 22, 2007; and Syed Shoaib Hasan, "Top Baloch Rebel Leader 'Killed'," *BBC News*, November 21, 2007, available from: *www.news.bbc.co.uk/go/pr/fr/-/2/hi/south_ asia/7106270.stm*, accessed on November 30, 2007. For an unusually impassioned Indian commentary on the killing, see B. Raman, "Baloch Che Guevara Is Dead: The Freedom Struggle Continues," Paper No. 2473, South Asia Analysis Group, November 23, 2007, available at *www.saag.org/papers25/paper2473.html*, accessed on November 26, 2007.

68. Rahimullah Yusufzai, "The Case Against Mengal," *The News*, September 9, 2007, available at *www.jang.com.pk/thenews/ sep2007-weekly/nos-09-092007/dia.htm#4*, accessed on September 13, 2007.

69. Senate of Pakistan, pp. 46-47.

70. *Ibid.*, pp. 95-101.

71. *Ibid.*, p. 100.

72. Interview by author in Pakistan in January 2007. Identity withheld on request. Emphasis is the author's.

73. ICG, *Pakistan: The Worsening Conflict in Balochistan*, p. ii.

74. Dunne, p. 68.

75. A number of major recent initiatives by the Pakistan government to protect Chinese nationals in Pakistan are outlined in Raman, "Security of Chinese Nationals in Pakistan."

76. Steven Metz, *Rethinking Insurgency*, Carlisle, PA: Strategic Studies Institute, U.S. Army War College, June 2007, pp. v-vi, available at *www.StrategicStudiesInstitute.army.mil*, accessed on September 24, 2007.

www.ingramcontent.com/pod-product-compliance
Lightning Source LLC
Chambersburg PA
CBHW031328290526
45784CB00014B/2439